YOU WERE BORN TO BE AN ENTREPRENEUR

The Mystery of Discovering your Calling and Career

Dr. Jeremy Lopez

YOU WERE BORN TO BE AN ENTREPRENEUR
By Dr. Jeremy Lopez
Copyright © 2014 by Jeremy Lopez

Published by Identity Network
P.O. Box 383213
Birmingham, AL 35238
www.identitynetwork.net
United States of America
The author can be contacted at customerservice@identitynetwork.net

Book design by
Treasure Image & Publishing
TreasureImagePublishing.com
248.403.8046

TABLE OF CONTENTS

CAREER AND CALLING

In speaking about career and calling, it is good to know that there is a career to which each is called. However, many don't realize that there's also a higher call or a calling that you also are required to move into in your life in God.

Let me break it down for you. We look at situations such as job versus vocation. How many of us work a job? Probably everyone. How many of you know that you are actually in your vocation? Probably not as many. There is a difference, because most people in society work jobs but they have no clue what their vocation, or calling is. The same is true for career and calling.

When we look at the life of a job, and answer *why* we're working in the job where we are, many say, "Well, it's the first thing that came along and I took it.... Well, it paid more money than the other job I was on...."

How many people in society take a certain job because one makes more money than the other? Many people do that, yet it doesn't make them happy. The old saying, "Money doesn't buy you happiness," is true. But if there is happiness and an internal joy within your heart--what I call "unspeakable joy"--money adds to that. When you are trying to look for more money as a means to happiness, you will not survive at any time in your life.

Most people work jobs and they think, "This is all I can do, because it makes the best money that I have ever made before in my life." Or many people look at themselves and pre-judge themselves maybe because they never had a college degree, or never knew what they were called to do, and all of a sudden they got hooked into something, and then maybe in two to four weeks they begin to learn and change the paradigm in their mind and begin to learn a new hobby-- or a new skill--and they realize, "This is what I'm called to do."

I know people who are in printing and got their first job within a month when they were twenty or eighteen. They learn how to do printing and twenty; thirty years later they are still into printing. There is nothing wrong with that. For many people it can be a career. But for some people it is just a job for them. Many people don't believe they can own businesses. Many people love their jobs, but they don't realize that their job is actually their career. We never stop to realize that a vocation is something that we are called to do.

JOB VERSUS VOCATION

When we are dealing with job versus vocation, we have to know that a job comes from the mind. It comes from reshaping and reformulating the mind to a new paradigm, and training the mind to get into gear with what we feel comfortable in doing. We call that our job.

However, a vocation is something that comes from within. It comes from your heart. A vocation is not something that has to be programmed by the mind as discipline the way a job does. A vocation comes from deep within your heart, or your spirit, where you know for certain you have found the vein of your life.

In the same way, we can contrast career versus calling. A career is a service we perform. We trade our time, effort, skill, knowledge, and experience for a salary, benefits or other income. Many people work a job because it offers great benefits, and that's wonderful, but we need to look a little deeper into things.

Let's continue with career. You may refer to it as your employment, your work, your livelihood, your occupation, your living, your trade, your vocation, your profession, or maybe it's just a job. Many people work just a job. You may have many reasons to go to work each day, but unless you are independently wealthy, earning an income is a primary career motive. You realize that in order to survive financially, you *need* to go to work, and work hard to make a living.

We have to know the difference between a career and a calling. Not many in society know their calling. As a life coach, I have more people coming to me saying, "I don't know what I am called to do in my life."

And I reply, "You have to look at the words you just said. 'I don't know what I'm *called* to do in my life.'"

The majority of the people that I talk to about a calling I ask, "Do you presently work?"

"Well, yeah I have a job."

"What are you looking for?"

Many people tell me, "Well I'm looking for another job."

"Well, guess what? You don't know what your *calling* is, and you will never know what your calling is." I respond. A calling is not a job because anyone can work a job. A job is something that a person goes out to get because they need to make money. That's a job. A calling is something that comes from within, as I stated earlier.

Your calling refers to a personal interest, maybe an attraction, a drive or a passion that is usually of a higher order. It isn't just something you *want* to do, but rather something you *need* to do.

Let me stop for a moment and explain what I mean when

I say it is something that you "*need*" to do. First of all, a calling is something that captures your imagination. It touches you deeply. It absorbs you, whether or not you can explain why.

Many people don't stop to realize that when dealing with a calling, it is something they say, "It's something I know I just *have* to do." When you go to a job, it's not necessarily something you *have* to do. (You *have to* with regard to making a living and surviving because you need to feed your family), but it's not something that <u>drives</u> you and makes you feel that if you don't accomplish it, it's a matter of life and death. It's a matter of your joy. It's a matter of something awakened in you saying, 'I know now this is why I was put here on planet earth.'

Now you can tell the difference between a job and a vocation, and the difference between a career and a calling. A calling is something you know you *have* to do, you *need* to do in order to find the ultimate, unspeakable joy you need in your life. It makes you say, "This is the real me."

How many work a job and realize that you're really not being the real you?

I talk with many people, those I coach or those that call me, and they say, "My job is something that I hate to do. I hate to answer the phone. I hate having to do accounting, and numbers just drive me crazy... but I'm good at it." It's frustrating when you look at the situation you realize that it's something that you pretty much just have to do because you need money. On the other hand, for some people owning an accounting firm is something that is their calling, their vocation, where they know they *have* to do it.

Why? It's back to job versus vocation. Where a job is where we go to work to get money to pay the bills, a vocation is from within. If it is someone has a *vocation* as an accountant, for example, they realize the purpose and the definition behind it says, "I'm not just here to make money." No, a vocation says, "I like to add these things up because of the fact that I am empowering someone else. When I'm doing accounting for my client, (Tina), it becomes my *mission*. There is a drive within me that makes me want to do this for her, because there is a greater desire to bless her, take care of her, supply her needs so that when I lay my head down at night I know I have empowered someone with what I *love* to do." See what I'm saying? It is something that touches you deeply. Something that goes beyond. Something that absorbs you, and you absorb it.

Understanding a Vocation

A calling may or may not earn an income, or it might become a career where it makes you millions of dollars. But let me ask you an honest question: *Are you willing to do something in your life where there will always be joy?* When you never come home dreading having to wake up in the morning and go to work? Many dread having to even think about their "job" during the day.

However, if it's your vocation you don't think, *"I can't wait for the clock to strike five to go home."* No, because it's something that you know is your **mission**. It goes beyond the border of your thinking and being all about *you.* It goes beyond the borders and reaches and extends out to millions upon millions of people that if you complete your vocation with love, passion, and desire then it goes beyond you. You are touching the world.

If everyone in society were working their vocation, imagine how the world and nations would be touched! We can touch the nations with joy.

Everyone that you come in contact with, for example, at Wal-Mart or Target, you will start to see more smiling faces. You will see the joy, and more people wanting to help you and go the extra mile with you.

There is a scripture that is very powerful that deals with this:

"Whoever hits you on the cheek, offer him the
other also; and whoever takes away your coat,
do not withhold your shirt from him either."
Luke 6:29

In other words, "If your brother asks for something, you give them extra. Give them the shirt off your back."

It is something that goes beyond trying to just do your job. When it's your heart, it goes beyond just giving them what they ask for, and you give them something greater; something that is more powerful saying, "I'm not just going to give you this, I'm going to give you that as well... I'm not just going to give you this information, I'm going to give you more information."

A calling may take the form of art or craft or other creative endeavors, such as writing, painting, playing a musical instrument. It may involve volunteer service, such as teaching. Volunteer services do not always guarantee you to have money. Volunteer services represent the fact that you are doing something because you *love* to do it for others, not just for yourself. The same is true of teaching, working with children or the elderly or doing a charitable work.

People wanting to make a difference in their community, or the world at large may be called to a religious order. I consider this moving out of vocation and into a higher spiritual call. It is something that goes beyond you as a person and reaches the masses of the universe; it reaches people all over the globe because you begin to realize that it's not about you, it's about other people. It's a higher call of service in your life.

You don't approach your call with some kind of militant mentality because someone is giving you orders to do it. No, you begin to be the one that is giving the orders to yourself saying, *"I am doing this."* Begin to move and command yourself so that you know as a General it is your passion to say, *"I've got to make sure everything is working properly because my heart is in it."* If your heart were not in it you wouldn't care if it moved properly; you would just do the minimum to get a paycheck and go home.

Your vocation goes beyond that limited mentality. It goes beyond one being there just to make money. It involves **life**: information, revelation, giving of your entire being to someone else. That's what a vocation does to someone. It says, *"I desire to give you more of me than just information."* Vocation is a powerful thing.

THE LABOR OF LOVE

People seldom recognize that a true calling is associated with serving others. A personal leisure activity such as golf, bowling, hunting, fishing, sewing, knitting or building miniature ships may fall into the realm of a hobby. However, if we end up performing or teaching these hobbies so that they can be shared with others, then our vocation may become both calling *and* career. The idea is to blend the two together so that it's not just something that you *have* to do, but something that you can make a career out of.

In other words, it's something that is buried deep within in you and you begin to say, "If I love this that much, I can actually make money with this."

According to universal principles like the law of attraction, truths found in the Word of God, and the many things that the Creator set into the universe as laws just for His people, did you know that money will follow what you love to do when you focus your attention and put your heart into it?

Let me put it to you another way: The Word of God says that, *"as a man thinketh in his heart, so is he,"* (Proverbs 23:7). In other words, whatever you love in your heart to do - good or bad - it is going to be attracted and drawn to you, according to the law of attraction. You are going to be performing or living out thoughts that are in your heart.

Imagine if your heart, love, and passion are behind and involved in your vocation. Consider it like baking a cake: you get all of the ingredients together, and begin adding them the bowl one after the other until the batter is finished. Then, all you have to do is put the pan of batter in the oven for it to go into the final stages of rising and transforming into to the final product. Every ingredient is essential for the good smell, right consistency and delicious taste of the cake. It works the same way for your vocation; if you have the right mixture of love, passion, imagination and creativity within you, the conditions are set and what you love will begin to create a masterpiece and rise to a finished work.

Examine your life and recognize that, no matter what you have a passion for, then blend it with your career. If you love to sew, or read, make it into a career. You might say, "How on earth can I make reading into a vocation? It's my hobby. I can't mix my hobby with my job." No! You have to change the way you think. Whatever you desire to do, whatever you are passionate about doing, put your hand to it because whatever you put your hand to will begin to prosper.

> *"The keeper of the prison did not look into*
> *anything that was under Joseph's hand,*
> ***because the Lord was with him; and***
> ***whatever he did, the Lord made it prosper."***
> *Genesis 39:23*

Whatever your heart is in is magnified because you are

walking in it and living it out. When its magnified, it is going to attract something of like-precious faith to it. It endeavors to attract something that is just like it. Its like a kindred-spirit; it draws something that is like it.

If I really enjoy reading, I can just consider it a hobby, place it in the back of my mind, and judge it by saying, "You will never make me money. You will never cause any productivity to happen in my life, but I enjoy reading on the side." However, what if I change my thinking and put my side-thing as my main thing?

I will begin to stir-up creativity and imagination with it and realize that, "If I really truly love doing this thing then maybe I need to expand the borders of my imagination and put it in a place where it could be my vocation."

"Whatever you do, work at it with all your heart, as working for the Lord, not for human masters..." Colossians 3:23 (NIV)

Look at people who love to fish. How do they make money? They get involved in fishing tournaments and it becomes their vocation because they love to do it. Whatever you love to do your heart will be in, and you will put integrity, excellence and the best quality behind it because it's in you to do it. It is the good thing in you that you love to do that puts a smile on your face, and you could do it for hours and days and weeks and months and years. It's your calling, not just a job.

If you look at the reading for example, how can you turn

reading into making money? If you're smart and you realize you can be a teacher and a student at the same time, and you know you are called to be an entrepreneur, then you can turn the efforts of reading into training other people how to read. You can begin to start schooling and classes, and using different creative techniques with your ability to begin to find a way to do what you love by getting others involved in it.

If something is truly your vocation, you will want to make sure other people know about what you love to do by involving them in it. You want to share that joy, passion, love and desire with other people. On the other hand, a job is something you don't want people involved with. You are just there for you, to get the money and go home. Your vocation will always be more than you. It will want to be able to speak out and say, "I want you to know what I love to do."

Think of this, if you're married and are madly in love with your spouse, you will want to tell people about the love of your life. Do you not? You want to display that person whenever you are in public; you are proud to be with them. "My wife looks beautiful. My husband is handsome. I want to show you off to my friends."

If you have found someone you are dating, what do you start doing when something is heading towards a strong commitment? You begin to take that person to your parents to show them who you are dating. You bring them home on holidays, you begin to show them to people you love and care for. That's the difference between a job and a vocation.

Whatever you love to do, you will want to show it off because you will want other people to be blessed by that thing that you love as well.

Remember, you're made in God's image and likeness. You have the creativity of the Creator's mind in you, so that you can expand your borders of your vision to transform your side-hobby into a lifestyle that can produce money and anything you need it to produce. It is in your blood to do it.

MERGING CAREER
WITH CALLING

We pursue a career primarily for income, but we pursue a calling primarily for satisfaction. However, if you love your career so much that you would do it for free, and you can afford to do so, it will likely become a calling as well. In the same way, if a calling begins to produce a good income, it has also become a career.

Why are such distinctions important to us? Because many of us cling to a calling but we struggle financially because we ignore or resist the need for a practical income-producing day-job. We've all heard of the person that says, "I must be free to follow my heart, and devote my life to my art," and they become a "starving artist" with no income. On the contrary, others among us focus so much on climbing a career ladder that we abandon the joy and life-affirming calling that might bring even more fulfillment and meaning to their lives.

Some of us have to realize that our career and calling have merged into one. That's one thing I have learned in my life. For others, they have remained separate and distinct. One way is not necessarily better than another. Yet we have to have our own unique process. For every person there is a process, and in that process your journey is going to be about

<u>you</u> and how you got there. You can't look at other peoples' lives and say, "You turned your hobby into this... I can do it the same way." Realize that you can't go the route other people have taken.

Many of us don't realize we suffer from a lack of knowledge. This is where a life coach is helpful to give you the knowledge and the wisdom you need to unlock the secrets about learning how to classify a job and a vocation; to distinguish between something that you will do for a living and something that you love to do. Too often we separate the two, but we need to realize that we are called to merge the two, like two sides of the same coin.

Whatever you love to do, you will work hard for and it will become your own spiritual job, for instance. Whatever you love to do, you will work hard to get the job done. You know it's not about the money, but living a life that is satisfying.

Do you want a life of satisfaction? Many of you will say, "Absolutely, I want a life of satisfaction. I want to look back on my life and know I did what I loved to do." That is the prize: To look at your life and be able to say that you love doing what you are doing. Many of us can't say that, although some of us can.

WHAT AWAKENS YOUR HEART?

I know many life coaches who love doing what they do because they love empowering others. It puts a smile on their face. They are satisfied to have people tell them, "Oh, wow that just really changed my life. It touched my life. It gave me hope and a bright future. It showed me something I could really do in my life." Would you love to live a life that is empowering to others?

Many of you love to put a smile on people's faces. Well, you don't have to be a life coach to do that. All you have to do is find and discover inwardly that treasure that has always been within your heart that is crying out for expression. It's dying for you to open it up and say that it is something you love to do. You are actually probably doing it all the time on side jobs, hobbies or things you don't normally pay attention to. But you need to pay attention to detail! Pay attention to things that you love doing subconsciously, but you don't recognize that it actually can be an important part of your every-day life, and bring you money and joy.

Unfortunately, some people would never consider waking up at 8:00 a.m. to do something that they actually love doing. Would you ever consider saying, "Today I'm not going to go to my job. I'm going to go down here and begin to take up shooting. I'm going to go help my neighbor clean up his yard. I'm going to go mow the grass for my aunt because I love cutting grass and I know that she needs it done, and it's just something that makes me feel good."

We begin to recognize that this pull or draw is something we need to give attention to because we love doing it. Pay attention to the detail!

Most people would say, "I'm taking off work today to do *this* because I love doing it, but I can't allow it to be top priority. I have to keep it on the back burner of my mind, and not bring it to the front. The front needs to be my job of survival. Today I'll take off work to do that and tomorrow I'll get back to the ball-and-chain. I get back to my job and something I have to do because I have to survive and live and have money."

If you live that way, every day of your life will be in that rut. That routine. But what if you let that treasure speak to you, and something in you awakens and asks, "What if... What if I took what I'm doing today that I enjoy and *make* it my job? What if I made a career of cutting grass?" You start to consider a pay scale of what you would charge for the services, like trimming bushes, planting flowers and raking leaves to give your clients a beautiful yard. How do you know if it's your career? Because it is something that draws and drives you.

Imagine you go down the street, you will notice the beautification awards signs that the city puts in people's yards because they are so breathtakingly beautiful. The flowers are beautiful, and the first thing that pops into your mind is, "Man, somebody did that job really well." If you stop there, you will dismiss anything else. You restrain your creativity and imagination, and you only admire the beauty of the handiwork of someone *else's* creativity. You will forget it and keep on going, and force your attention on what you don't like doing... your job.

But let's try this again: If you let yourself stop in your car and look at the landscape and that beautification award and the yard, and instead of just admiring someone else's work, your creativity and imagination are stirred. All of a sudden you begin to say to yourself, "Wait a minute, I could do that too... I could put my heart into this work and make it top-notch that people will want to pay me. They will pay me above and beyond what a young kid would charge because it is my passion, not just a summer job. Or maybe the elderly lady is in her yard planting roses because she wants so badly to have a beautiful yard, and I could use my passion to help her to make her yard as beautiful as she wants it, and she would gladly pay me for my services."

Pay attention to what catches your attention. Take a step back and say, "That yard that was breathtaking... That yard that was so beautiful... These yards that I am always paying attention to as I'm driving to my ball-and-chain job... What if what I love to view and look at was my *living*? What if *that* was my job? What if that is something that I become the head of? What if that is something that I become the leader of? If that were mine, I could make killer money off of it. I'm doing what I love to do and making other people's lives better by changing their yards forever and bringing a smile upon their face."

"Does not wisdom cry out, And understanding
lift up her voice?" Proverbs 8:1

Realize that life doesn't pass you by: Life is always in your face saying, "Look at me. Pay attention to me!" How often we miss it. Life is in the details and we need to pay attention to those details even on your way to the ball-and-chain. This will cause us to slow down, stop, look and listen. It happens every day of our lives and we never stop to look, never stop to listen to something in creation calling out to us as a voice saying, "Hey look! Look this way. Look in this direction. You love looking at this, but I need you to pay attention to the detail of the beautiful thing you are paying attention to."

Only then, we will then begin to recognize that something outside of your job has been calling you all of your life. You take a big step of faith and dare yourself to do it. As you step out, something awakens in you: **your calling**. It is no longer a hobby, but is now a career. Now it is called a vocation. Now it is a lifestyle that will overflow in any and every area of your life.

THE OVERFLOW OF A FULFILLED LIFE

If you are just working a job, you will get whatever you were hired to be paid. Nothing more, nothing less. And if you're fortunate--maybe once a year at Christmas--you will get a good bonus, but don't count on it.

A vocation and a call is always validated with an overflow. If you're in a vocation and a calling, God orchestrates the universe and creation to say, "This man or woman is constantly pondering and putting their love, their passion, devotion and desire behind what they are doing, so go get them. Go on that same high-frequency level that says passion and desire." It begins to send that same wavelength, or frequency of the universe that God has orchestrated. Whatever you think about, that same thing will be drawn to you, and something in you becomes alive again because you have connected to the same frequency level of what you love to do.

*"God [who] is able to do **immeasurably more**
than all we ask or imagine, **according to his
power that is at work within us...**"*
Ephesians 3:20

Before you know it something will be drawn to you

saying, "What if I began to do what I love to do. I'm noticing that the more I pay attention to what I love to do, the more it is attracted to me and I see more of it around me. It is surrounding me and it's like a circle around me that everywhere I look, I see the thing I love to do."

Whatever you focus upon, love and desire you will thrust yourself into and it will begin to grow in you. Not like a virus that's bad and you have to have medication to get rid of. It begins to grow and have life. Everything in you will wake up to say, "This is the real me. This is a lifestyle. This is me. This is the reason why I was put here on planet earth." Something in you begins to wake up.

Only you can decide.

PAY ATTENTION!

I remember a long time ago being in school and having the teachers say, "Hey! Pay attention! Wake up! Listen to what I'm saying." My teachers knew that if I didn't pay attention, my grades would suffer.

Similarly, our life suffers when we don't pay attention to those who have the wisdom that we need in our lives. There will always be people in your life who will have more or know more than you. God sends these people to our life because He knows they have the answers that we need. He knows that they have a truth that will set us free. It's a key to unlocking our understanding. They'll bring that "A-HA!" moment, and the answers we have been seeking. They bring wisdom to touch your life and set you free, which means it will put you in another dimension and a new way of living. The key that these key people bring open you to a new reality where your life steps-up to the plate, and you hit home-runs! They bring you up higher to score.

When someone says to pay attention, what they are saying is that you have to be disciplined in your mind and body. When someone is not paying attention that means their mind is wandering off, they are nodding off, and everything becomes off. You are knocked off the course of everything you are supposed to focus on and pay attention to.

When we don't focus or pay attention, it affects our vision and growth. Your visionary mind has ingrained in it who you are and what you are supposed to be doing all the rest of the days of your life, but when we lose focus, our vision begins to deteriorate and diminish our growth. If you don't care for and give attention to that which God has intended for you to be, to walk in, and to accomplish, then it will begin to deteriorate.

Everything in life must be fed. Everything in life must be nurtured. There is not one thing on planet earth that does not require attention, or some type of nurturing, nutrition, watering, and focus. Life is created for growth through some type of joint supply that will cause it go into a higher state of being, to progress beyond where you are. Everything is that way.

> *As a result, we are no longer to be children,*
> *tossed here and there by waves and carried*
> *about by every wind of doctrine, by the trickery*
> *of men, by craftiness in deceitful scheming; but*
> *speaking the* **truth in love, we are to grow up**
> *in all aspects into Him who is the head, even*
> *Christ, from whom the* **whole body, being**
> **fitted and held together by what every joint**
> **supplies,** *according to the proper working of*
> *each individual part,* **causes the growth of the**
> **body for the building up of itself in love.**
> *Ephesians 4:14-16*

We were created as human beings to love and to be

loved. We were created to never want to be alone. There is not one person on planet earth who really desires, from the moment they are born to the day that they die, to be alone, never to be in public, never to be with anyone. You might say, "Well I know this girl down the street who is married and they tend to stay to themselves a lot." It's not a problem. They still have each other. It is in our DNA to want to be able to mingle with people, co-labor with people, whether it is one, two or a thousand. The networking process in the universe will continue until the day we die. There is always a networking of who you meet, and you will make a decision if they are going to stay in your life or go.

ALL ARE CALLED

We are spending some time here talking about paying attention and staying focused, because all too easily people will get off course of what they are called to do. When you get off course, you lose your footing, get distracted, and you get into another world. You get into wanting to do something else, be something else, move over here, move over in that arena, trying to keep up with the Joneses, trying to accomplish or have whatever everyone else around you has instead of to focusing on what you should be doing pertaining to the call of God upon your life.

Everyone in creation has a call. Every person is created with an objective (a purpose), as well as an obstacle. You cannot have an object of focus without having an obstacle. This is because life is not free for you.

One of the things I tell people all the time if you understand from the Bible, nothing is free. Salvation is not free. Salvation costs your entire life. Everyone talks about *freely given*, but something that is freely given does not mean it is free. That means it is freely given. There is always a cost to everything.

Freedom is not free. It cost someone's life to fight for that freedom. It costs something. Freedom and liberty do not come because they are freedom and liberty. They come with a price tag to them. Every objective that you are trying to achieve and accomplish in life will always have an obstacle attached to it that you will have to overcome.

Overcoming is the price.

*"But in <u>all these things</u> **we overcome**, because of him that hath loved us." Romans 8:37*

The definition of the words, "victor" or "overcomer" indicate that there is obstacle that must be overcome. An overcomer has to "come over" something. As an overcomer, you are going to have to go through the fire and come out on the other side unscathed.

You are always going to have to go through ridicule to see if when you are tested you come out true on the other side; not to see if you are "worthy enough," but to see if you qualify because you focused on the goal and you did not let the ridicule affect you.

Many people are not truly <u>hungry enough</u> for the goal and vision set for their lives to accomplish it. They easily deviate from it and they don't pay attention. The goal does not burn within them because it hasn't been cared for, fed, or cultivated. It hasn't been given the proper attention, so it doesn't become a driving force in their life and decisions.

Since their goal does not drive them, and transform into their lifestyle or the object of their affection, then obstacles seem insurmountable.

These obstacles take the form of ridicule, or mental torment, which comes from people's words, or your own insecurities that make you feel like you don't have enough money to achieve your goal, you don't have friends to empower you, you don't have leaders that will lead you, or you don't have the right tools to prepare to build it.

If you think like this, then the obstacle has gotten you, and your hunger and your drive for the object of your affection has been extinguished.

Don't Focus on the Obstacles – Focus on the Goal

Any time you have a focus on a goal or achievement, if it is a God-given goal, it will drive you and you won't be satisfied or happy until that goal is officially achieved and is stamped with a seal of approval. You can ride in it, you can look at it, you can live it out, and you can actually understand it more because it will manifest in your reality in your world. That is when you know it was the object of your affection. It was the object of the focus which God has intended for you to walk in since the very beginning of the foundations of the world. That is when you know you have overcome. That is when you know you have achieved everything you need to achieve.

> *"Not as though I had already attained, either were already perfect: but I follow after, if that I* ***may apprehend <u>that</u>*** *for which also I am apprehended of Christ Jesus.... **I press toward the goal for the prize of the upward call of God in Christ Jesus.***"*
> *Philippians 3:12, 14*

Is there an objective there? Is there an object there? Is there an obstacle there? All three, absolutely there is.

Because there is an objective and there is an object of affection, an object of a goal, and object of focus which is the end of the race. The obstacle may be getting tired. Can you keep up with the fact that your legs get tired when you are running? Running is not something that is fun. Running is a disciplinary act. It is something that you know in order for a runner or a jogger to win the race, achieve their accomplishments, and see if they can come in first place or second place or third place, they KNOW that they are going to go through a lot of sweat and a lot of blood and tears. They are going to have to practice and practice and practice. And when they get in the marathon, when they start running the race, their legs are going to hurt, their muscles are going to ache, they are going to get hot under the sun, their bones are going to start aching and their body is going to start losing fluid if they don't fill it up as they run. That is why you see the people on the sidelines giving the runners water because their fluids are escaping fast.

You do have obstacles there. In order to achieve what you need to achieve, the obstacle must be conquered. Obstacles are always present, but you can't let them discourage you. In the Kingdom of God, anytime you have a focus or a call upon your life with the drive to make sure it is completed - whether it is a call of God, whether it is an entrepreneurship adventure, whether it is something you have to achieve on your job - if it is something that drives you, it will be almost like a stake in your heart from God that says, "I'm not going to remove this until you do it." In other words, the call has penetrated your heart so completely that it must be fulfilled. You put your mind, will and emotions behind it.

When you make this commitment to the call or goal, you will find that you will begin to see the obstacle appear. When you feed your call or the goal which lies before you with the attention, hunger, drive and love - then and only then will the obstacle begin to appear.

> *"In this world you will have trouble. **But take heart!** I have overcome the world." John 16:33*

When you were a kid, did you get one of those coloring books that aren't really coloring books, but you highlight over one thing and you begin to see a hidden picture underneath it. And the more you highlight it or scratch the covering off, you begin to find the secret code behind it that could not be revealed unless you put action behind your faith or the movement. You could not see the picture that was underneath it until you actually put your heart or your affection into the marker to begin to rub, to begin to highlight it, and that is when you begin to see it appear.

That is the "obstacle." Anytime you begin to put action and faith and your emotions, and you begin to project your affection, emotion and love into the call that God has for you, your intimacy begins to develop. Your passion begins to be developed towards that thing that God has put before you to accomplish, achieve, desire and consume. That is when the obstacle begins appearing the most. It knows that you have become serious about your call.

Let's think of it in terms of a relationship: when two

people get serious with one another, at first they are flirting, dating and are just having fun together. Everything is rosy, no one sees anything negative or bad. Everything is wonderful, and the couple gets like a "puppy-love" mentality. Even though they've only had a couple dates, they begin thinking, "Wow, I could be with this person forever."

But as the couple gets more serious and goes deeper into the relationship, obstacles begin to surface. "Oh, I didn't realize that she doesn't put the cap back on the toothpaste. I didn't realize that he could be a little annoying at times..." All of the pet-peeves begin to come to light. They become potential obstacles in the relationship and must be addressed.

THE HIDDEN TREASURE

The more devoted you become to the call of God and it becomes the object of your affection, the more you will begin to notice obstacles surface in your life. The deeper you step into something, even from the beginning, you will desire to understand it more. It's like the more you taste it, the more your hunger and craving for it intensifies. It is then that you begin to see the good, the bad and the ugly of it. You begin to understand how it functions and flows and you also begin to understand the hurdles necessary get to the place where it will function and flow easily.

When you look for treasure, what do you do? You are going to have to go through a lot of stuff to discover it. You have maps that lead you to this ocean... to that place... to that old castle... to down there at the bottom of the mountain... down the valley... then dig under this rock.

A pirate that goes to seek out treasure is going to be faced with a lot of obstacles. The more that he begins to get the passion and the drive to search for the treasure, (because he knows it's valuable; he knows it's what he needs), he will begin to understand that he must face obstacles and seek help to overcome them.

He decides to use the map. He determines that no matter how frustrated he gets and wants to give up, he will press on.

Maybe the obstacle is he doesn't understand the ancient map full of rips and tears or the paper has turned brown with age.

The pirate still understands, "It is going to be hard because I am going to face a lot of obstacles, but the treasure is worth the trouble."

Now, what about you? What is the strongest in your life? That is a question you have to ask yourself. Is the obstacle stronger than the object of your affection (the will of God, the passion of God, the gift of God in you)?

What will you do?

You Have What it Takes

I can tell you numerous amounts of people that I have carried through life coaching and talked to and prophesied to, and so many people say, "I have a business idea and I am going to go for it. I'm excited." But the first time the obstacle begins to raise its ugly head to them, they lose their focus. Instantly.

They begin to think, "Well, maybe it wasn't God. Maybe it is something that I can't achieve. Maybe it's something that really wasn't for me. Maybe it was somebody else's idea."

They begin to question if it was really God in the first place. They begin to question if it was too powerful for them to accomplish and achieve. "Maybe it was just never for me from the beginning."

What happens is, their passion wasn't STRONG ENOUGH in the area of the focus that God has presented to them.

God will only _present_ it to you. God will not say, "I am going to force you to fall in love with it." He won't say, "I'm going to make sure that you are fully equipped to do what you are called to do."

<u>Along the path</u> is where God will begin to equip you.

"His divine power hath given unto us all things
that pertain unto life and godliness, through the
knowledge of Him that hath called us to glory
and virtue." 2 Peter 1:3

Although you have inside of you everything pertaining to life and godliness, you must still be equipped. You already have the tools in you. The problem is that you are not conscious of those tools. You are not aware, and you easily forget that you already have everything it takes to achieve that goal, and have good success. You have the tools to make it happen, and you will discover them and learn to work with them along the path of life. The whole time God has said you already have it because He has already given it; you are just <u>now</u> receiving it.

God says, "You have always had what it takes. I never ever give a focus, or I never deliver the call of God on your life without first-and-foremost before the foundation of the world, empowering you, impregnating you with every tool you need, with everything that will supply you to get you where you need to be going. I also prepare you and give you the tools you need to sustain it once you get down the road."

*"But we have this **treasure in earthen vessels**,*
that the excellency of the power may be of God,
and not of us." 2 Corinthians 4:7

Once you get to the Omega state of being, (which is the ending of something), finally moving into your object of affection, into the call, into the gift, then you begin to understand that God has empowered you before the foundations of the earth to maintain, sustain, and cause the call to grow.

There is a growth formula buried deep inside of the treasure within your earthen vessel; this growth is called to equip, sustain, and maintain everything in your life, including your call and your gift. Whatever it is you have in you, it has been in there before you were ever born. Before you were ever conscious that you were alive, it was already in you. It has always been in you.

> *"It is the glory of God to conceal a matter; to search out a matter is the glory of kings."*
> *Proverbs 25:2*

In this life, because our minds has been limited and we are constantly learning. God has given us, as kings, the privilege of searching out what has been hidden. As you grow in life, you begin to approach your calling and you begin to say, "Now I am getting the hands on what I need," (in reality, you had them the whole time), but to you they are fresh. To you, you are just now getting what you already had.

> *"I can do all this through him who gives me strength." Philippians 4:13*

You can do it. The only thing you need to determine is whether or not the drive in you is stronger to quit more than it is to continue. Is the *obstacle* in you too big, or is the *object* bigger? Which one do you love the most?

Once you fall in love with somebody, they are all you think about. When you fall in love with someone, your affection, your mind, your attention all day long at work focuses on that person you fell in love with. You become a dreamer. You dream about marrying them. You dream about being with them, and your focus has automatically shifted and nothing else matters in your life.

That is the place you need to come to when focusing upon the gift, the call of God upon your life: **nothing else should matter**. It is the love of your life, and one day you want to marry that call. You want to engage in it, and *become* it because it has always been in you and has always been a part of you. That is why you feel as if you are finally meeting your first love. You are finally meeting the love of your life. You are finally meeting that which you know you have always been a part of, what you have always been looking for all of your life. That is the focus of your call, and how you should feel.

FLEXIBILITY FOR GROWTH

What is bigger to you: the object or the obstacle?

When we focus on paying attention, being disciplined, getting to the place you know you need to be, I want to give you a couple points of things you need to remember in paying attention and focusing on your call.

That is the first thing you have to do is get over your lack of flexibility. Flexibility is a key ingredient to your success. This does not contradict keeping your eyes focused on the prize, or your drive and love for the call God has given you. While it is necessary to know what you want and to be specific in your goals and plans, it is also vital to be flexible in your approach. Always remember that.

It is absolutely crucial that you periodically review all of the pieces of your process. You may even need to reconsider and change the ultimate goal itself.

What I am saying is, you need to be flexible enough to allow the goal to change and grow. Anytime you look at something and say, "That is what I want to accomplish. That is in me to do. That's my goal. That's my career. That's the love of my life..." then you must be flexible enough to know that object you are talking about will shift and change. And you have to love it through its growth. Love it through its change, and love it with the understanding that it will multiply and produce for you.

Using the example of a relationship again, if you fall in love with somebody and at first you have that image, (their beautiful eyes, their long hair, etc.) ingrained in your spirit, you have a visual of what they look like. You focus on the image of them all day long and you can't wait to be with them. That image you are getting there is how they look in the now; It's not how they are going to look ten years, or even one year from now.

This is because that goal that you are ultimately trying to achieve to get your hands on will shift within a year. It will look different, it will grow and it will act different. But you have to realize that that's life and it's okay to allow yourself and it to grow together. You don't want a goal that you look at right now and say, "I love it," and then twenty years down the road it has changed on you and then you don't like it or embrace it anymore. The bottom line is, you want things to produce.

Let's say, for example, a man falls in love with a girl, but he sets so much affection on a particular aspect of her appearance: "I love you because you have blonde hair. It's long. I love that you weigh 125 pounds, and you talk like this, you dress like this." Well, that's great that he loves her and those things that he sees about her, but if he is not flexible in his object of affection, if he is not flexible in what he sees before his eyes, he is going to stunt her growth. All the days of her life she is going to live in misery and depression trying to keep that same amount of weight, or that same hair color. Everyone knows hair color will change and eventually probably turn grey or fall out or whatever. And she will never be able to cut her hair, and she will always have to dress when she is seventy like she's twenty years old again.

When I look at my business, when I look at ministry, and I look at my life I don't focus on something and say, "I love what I see at this moment because that's how it is going to be the rest of my life." No, I look at something and say, "Yes, I love what I see, but I am also going to love it ten years when it looks differently. I am also going to love it as it grows and expands because I am going to grow with it, and ultimately that goal is going to be a place of great expansion like the universe. I am going to expand with it, I am going to grow with it, and I am going to enjoy every moment of it."

Therefore, do I have the outcome of what the vision looks like in my spirit? Do I have the outcome of the object of my affection as more of my focus because I am flexible to add a little creativity and imagination to that?

Absolutely. That is what I want to focus on. Not necessarily loving what I see at the moment, even though I do, but giving it grace and room enough to say, "And you will change in looks, and you will change in size and you will change in personality, you will change in how you bring me back money. Instead of a Ma-and-Pa business you are going to expand and you are going to bring me a corporation. You are going to bring me a chain of stores."

You can't love how it looks without also being flexible. If you lack in flexibility, you will stunt its growth. You will never allow it to fully grow to its potential.

If you are not flexible, you will stunt the growth of your calling, you will damage it, you will depress it, and you will cause it not to produce for you in the way it was designed to.

FALLING IN LOVE
WITH THE VISION

I use the example of relationships when talking about your calling because it's something everyone can relate to. In a natural relationship, we realize that we are not here to control or to manipulate. It's the same with the calls of God on your life, no matter if it is entrepreneurship, becoming a minster, achieving goal like building a homeless shelter or passing the Bar Exam. When you see these callings in the perspective of a human relationship as a type-and-shadow, we can easily see what can do and how it can hurt us. We can see in the natural how inflexibility can hurt people and relationships, imagine what it would do to the call of God upon our lives.

People function and flow in the same way as goal-oriented visions. Although you can never physically stunt the growth of a person, your inflexibility and limited vision will bring oppression and bondage to them. When this happens, they will never be happy, and they will never produce to their fullness because you have stolen their joy, their laughter, the grace to expand and to gracefully mature. Relationships don't need to be controlled or oppressed. They need to be nurtured. If they gain a little weight, give them grace. If they lose a little weight, give them grace. That is sowing flexibility. When you fill a person full of flexibility and you love them for who they are, (the same way you would treat a goal or a vision), then that thing or that person will produce for you. Unspeakable joy from the inside of you will always cause a person to want to properly and healthily produce. They will produce healthy things for you and begin to expand with you.

"One gives freely, yet grows all the richer;
another withholds what he should give, and
only suffers want. Whoever brings blessing will
be enriched,   and one who waters will himself
be watered." - Proverbs 11:24-25

Please remember that every time you allow your goal grace to remove lack, you give power to be flexible with its growth. If you have your eyes on something that is a goal, you have to give it room to grow and room for you to grow with it. Give it grace. It has to be flexible.

That doesn't mean your eyes are off the goal; that means you see past what it is now and you see how big it will become in the future. You will be so lodged in the center of the greatness of what it is going to be become, you will get lost in it, and it will produce for you and give you the overflow that you have been looking for.

What you want is the overflow. Correct? You don't want something to look the same ten years from now as it does right now. You want to be in the midst of the *overflow*. Always focus on your vision and your goal. Don't necessarily see it for what it looks like now.

Fall in love with the outcome, what it is going to do, and what it is going to produce for you. Fall in love with the beauty of the wholeness and the entity of the call itself. Fall in love with the goal itself, the object itself, and the person itself. Fall in love with the wholeness of it so that you give it room to be flexible, give it grace to grow because you are going to grow with it.

Anytime you love something and your affection is projected towards it, you will always, always, always be joyful and gracious in growing with it. That way you can "grow old together," and yet you will love it as much as when you first fell in love with it.

It is the same way with your goal, your vision, your business. Do I love my business? Absolutely. I am in love with my business. I love what I do. I love everything about it. Is there an obstacle to attaining it all the time? Absolutely!

There's an obstacle, but the obstacle begins to be put in its proper place and therefore it knows where it stands. My affection for the wholeness, or the whole entity, of the business is far greater than my attention to the obstacle. The obstacle is not my problem anymore. Does it still raise its ugly head because it has to? Yes. It has to, because it keeps me on my toes to know where my passion is and to keep my love excited.

People always say in a relationship, "You are going to have to have a little fire in that relationship. You are going to have to have a little adventure to make it work." That is so true. No one wants to be in a relationship where there is not a lot of fire going on, there's not a lot of adventure going on, not a lot of unexpected miracles happening, unexpected joy sessions to break through, such as surprising dinners, surprising movies, joking around, surprising the other person with something you know they like to do. That's why Christmas and birthdays are so popular to people. Because everyone that loves giving gives surprises to those they love.

So keep the fire going. Keep the flame burning. You have to keep your first love stirred-up, whether its with your business, your call, your entrepreneurship, or relationship with your spouse. Always stoke the fire of passion. Every time you do, the obstacle will still be there, but will become lesser and lesser important to you. It will be easier to overcome because of the strength and motivation that comes with that passion.

Obstacles won't discourage you because you will understand that they are not the object of your affection. Everything is put in its proper place.

Believe it or not, God is the one that will put the obstacle there. God will put it there to keep you stirred-up to make sure your passion for what you are looking for is truly in the right place. If the fire ever goes out, the fire usually goes out when the obstacle is removed.

Is that not true? If there is nothing to fight, if there is nothing there to overcome, then what is the point of even having a passion for it? What is the point of ever truly getting the anticipation to jump over the fence if you know that something over the fence is something that you are going to love? If there isn't a fence there, you won't respect what you are looking for. You will not truly honor the goal, you will not truly honor the focus, and you will not truly have joy hit you when you reach it. If there is nothing to cause you to go down a narrow road to grab hold of it, you won't truly appreciate it when you get there.

STAY RECEPTIVE

Another aspect of staying flexible in achieving your goal is to stay receptive. It is very important because when you stop yourself from being flexible, you stop everything else around you from moving as well. It actually hinders those things that are trying to project and bring to you the help you need. Did you know that?

To help accomplish or achieve that, God uses creation to get you where you need to be. God uses everything in creation to help get you where you need to be. You need to make sure that you keep your flexibility intact. You need to make sure you are always very receptive in the situation. Always be a receiver and to receive from anyone and everyone that is there to help empower you.

Many people try to divert you from your call and from your goal, and you will know the difference. With discernment you will know who is in your life that is drawing you and pushing you further into your goal, and those who are there to divert you from it. Who is there in your life that is trying to get your eyes off the prize, and who is in your life saying, "Focus more on it. I have great news towards it. I have great ideas that will help empower you more to help make your goal happen."

Always surround yourself with healthy people. The

problem with most people is they don't know how to surround themselves with healthy, wholesome people. If a person is not whole (I didn't say perfect), they are not going to be much use to you. If a person is fragmented and stays that way and never gets treatment for it, it will ultimately take them down and take you with them. You cannot be positive around a bunch of negative people. You can't ever find your life at a place where you're growing, yet you are surrounded by people who are stagnant. It doesn't happen. You will be the one who will be taken down.

So you always need to make sure that you are receptive to those around you that you know you can approve of. Everything and anything in my life, I approve of. I want to make sure this worthy to be in my life. (This is not a prideful or arrogant stance, but rather a valuing of the gift of God within you.) Ask yourself, Is this someone who I can feed off of and they can feed off of me? Can we take each other to a higher plane in God? To a higher level of what we are trying to accomplish and achieve.

"As iron sharpens iron, so a man sharpens the countenance of his friend." Proverbs 27:17

Iron sharpens iron. You need to be receptive to those around you that you have placed the seal of approval on, and have proven being worthy enough to be there. What happens is you begin to sharpen one another, and you take each other higher and higher. You begin to sharpen their edges. You begin to sharpen the things in their lives that are keeping them bound with heavy weights trying to accomplish their goal... that God-given goal. And they will do the same for you. There is a difference between someone who allows you to lose focus and "fall asleep at the wheel," and someone who says, "Hey look, pay attention. You need to get your eyes back on this. Have you ever considered doing this? Going to class? If you go to a computer class it will help push you in the direction to achieve your goal in becoming a computer analyst. Have you ever considered going to law school?"

"And let us consider one another in order to stir up love and good works," Hebrews 10:24

These people will fan the flame of your passion, and stir you up to not give up. They begin to cut off the edges to say, "You need to go to law school. You can't have what you're looking for in your business until you have that law degree. It will do this for you and that for you. It will help save you a lot of money one day." You have to let people sharpen you, because most people who are helping you want to sharpen you.

Never fill your life full of "Yes-People." Fill your life full of people who sometimes disagree with you, yet always have your best interests at heart. People who always want the very best for you; not what they want, but what they know you are looking for. They can help put you there, but make sure they are honest with you and walk in integrity themselves. When you analyze their lives, they should be doing what they tell you they are going to do. They let their "yes" be yes and their "no" be no. They are people you can learn from by watching their lives.

If you have people in your life that you are not learning from and you constantly find yourself coaching them, pulling them back in line, causing them to pay attention, to not nod-off, you have to go rescue them down the street because they are in places they shouldn't be, you need to find yourself detaching from those people. If they are not willing to change and shift, I encourage you to love them with all that is in you. Love people regardless of who they are and where they are. Sometimes in life you have to detach yourself because maybe you are not the one who is supposed to lead them the rest of the way.

Do not be deceived: "Evil company corrupts good habits." 1 Corinthians 15:33

Moses and Joshua were that way. Moses was a great deliverer of the Israelites that were captive in Egypt. God used Moses to bring them out of Egypt, but He used Joshua to bring them into the Promised Land. Moses accomplished what God had for him to do, then Joshua took over. Joshua had to do what he had to do, and he needed to start when he needed to start. Not prematurely, making sure that he continued until God said it was done.

When you know in your heart you hear that voice that says, "It is accomplished. It is achieved. It is done," make sure you know when to walk away. The Kenny Rogers song that I always tell people in my life-coaching sessions when it comes to discernment: *You got to know when to hold 'em, know when to fold 'em, Know when to walk away and know when to run.*

You've got to have discernment to know when it is your time to leave, your time to stay, your time pour in, or your time to pull back. You need to ask yourself, "What is my time? What is my season? And in this season, what am I called to do? What am I called to give? What am I called to say? Am I called to be, or am I called to activate? Am I called to take a step backwards, or am I called to walk away? Or am I called to initiate?"

IRON SHARPENS IRON

You have to know what season you are in your life, and when you are dealing with people in your life you have to know and be guaranteed that those around you are there to challenge you as you challenge them. Is iron sharpening iron? Are they there for your best interest, or are they pulling something from you that will be for their best interest?

You are going to have to remember that if you want to reach your goal one day, you are going to have to receive from those that God has put in your life and allow their voices to empower you. You might say to yourself, "How do I know if their voice is speaking to me and helping me toward my goal?" When someone speaks to you, what they say should always empower you to think. If a person says something to you and they try to strip away the power for you to think about it, chew on it and meditate on it, then they are manipulating you. They are trying to override your thinking and want you to jump on their bandwagon of what they're thinking. They are trying to get off your roller coaster and get on theirs thinking, "Do what I tell you to do. When I say move you move."

In other words, anyone that ever takes away the power for you to think and allow what he or she are saying to be a challenge to you and to make your own decisions, is not a person you need in your life. Anything anyone has ever brought to my attention in my life, positive or negative, I make sure they have always left it where I have the power to think it over and then decide. A person who loves you and truly cherishes you would never take away the power for you to make your own decision, and take the power from you to ponder, outweigh the good and the bad and find out what is beneficial in what he or she has presented to you. You should think, "is it more effective to go the route that they have suggested, or is it more powerful for me to walk away from that?" Either way, the words that someone speaks to you will always empower you if they have your best interest at heart and only want the good for you. These people will see your vision and try to feed into it more, and not for selfish gain. They will always make you feel empowered.

Make sure you are one that is always receptive. Never let it be said about you that you have a lack of flexibility or receptivity. Always be receptive to those who God brings into your life, this way you will know they are there for a reason; they are there to help you not to hurt you. They are there to empower you. They don't just agree with what I am doing, if they love you they will share with you how they view and see what you are doing, keeping you and your best interests in mind. They will have no selfish-gain or strings attached. Their honesty will bring blessings back to them. If you love that person, you want your vision to be empowering to you and to them.

You want anyone and everyone in your life, that when you achieve your goal, through God's limitless love, you will want anyone attached to you to also be empowered. That's what makes me feel good. Whenever I get a new vision or a goal from God, I automatically think, "How will this empower my family? I can imagine that my friends will love this because it will work for them as well. I can make enough money to help them. I can make enough money to help my family." Instantly my mind shifts to how everyone who is connected to me in my life will be affected by it.

That is what you want to focus on. A man who focuses on giving out of their vision is one who will always be empowered and never suffer lack. You will suffer lack anytime you take your eyes off the prize of what the goal can do for you and everyone around you. Goals, callings, giftings and the vision have never been about "me, myself and I."

If they are from God they are for everyone, and you just happen to be the vessel God has chosen to take the reins of it and multiply it. Feed into it and make it big. Nobody can do it like you can, that's why God gave it to you.

TAKE ACTION

I talk a lot about the law of attraction. The law of attraction is scientific proof. It is not a religion thing, it's not a new age thing, and it's not a physic thing. It's a truth.

"As a man thinketh in his heart, so is he."
Proverbs 23:7

If you know my teachings, you know I refer to this scripture often because it is a powerful scripture. A decision that someone makes has first-of-all been present in their thought process. They thought it and it became their reality. Thoughts became things.

"Death and life are in the power of the tongue:
and they that love it shall eat the fruit thereof."
Proverbs 18:21

In the law of attraction, did you notice that at the end of the word "attraction" is the word "*action*"? This eludes to the fact that in order for you to begin to move into what you have been called to do, you have to have action. The problem with most people, especially Christian people, (and I see this all the time) is that they're always asking, "What is God going to do for me? When is God going to do?" You know what I tell them? I hate to break their hearts, but I tell them, "God's already done His part. He's waiting on you. God has already given you everything that pertains to life and godliness. He has already given you the tools and the weaponry you need to accomplish, achieve, succeed, outdo, undo anything and everything in life you need to do. Now He is waiting on you to move." The best thing you can tell a Christian is that, "God is done. Now it's time for you to arise."

When Christ was on the cross He said, "It is finished." What I share with people is that means it is finished for Him, and it's just beginning for you. He's done His part. It is the Omega state of His life here on earth. He has won the race in that area. He is finished, He's accomplished; now it's your turn to start your life as a co-creator. When Jesus died on the cross, you instantly became co-creator with Him. Immediately you began to receive the creativity, the inventions and everything that He had and died for. It is impregnated in you to finish what was started.

Therefore you have to have an action with your faith. Anytime you feel you need to do something, don't find yourself slapping God in the face by saying, "God when are you going to do it? I'm waiting for you to do something, God. I'm sitting back waiting for you." When God is saying, "I've been waiting on you this whole time."

*"For as the body without the spirit is dead, so
faith without works is dead also." James 2:26*

Faith without works is dead. This means faith without corresponding action won't work. You have to have action.

If you are in love with someone and they are all you think

about, how many times have you picked up the phone to call them and hung up? A person who is in love with something or somebody will always put action behind that love to try and reach it, to try and get closer, or try to be creative with that object of their affection.

You have to realize that there has to be action behind your faith. There has to be an action, a corresponding action with your vision. If you don't have one, your vision will die. It will not get accomplished, it will not be achieved, or it will be put off further and further into the future. The more you push your vision further into the future, you are pushing it without action. You are pushing it away without completing the action to bring it nearer to you. It's going to be pushed further into the future if you don't draw it with a rope of action.

Action puts a rope around your goal and draws it closer to you. If you don't have action behind your faith, you don't have a rope to draw the vision closer to you. You have to have the rope that draws it closer to you. Without the rope of action, you will never accomplish nor achieve. It will never be completed in your life. You must remember, "I always need to have the rope." Look in your hands constantly, "I've got the rope." Now begin to draw it closer to you. Put action behind it and it will draw close to you.

"Draw near to God and He will draw near to you." James 4:8

You see, God is actually asking you to draw close to Him

<u>first</u>. If you draw to Him, then He will draw to you. But He won't draw to you if you don't draw to Him.

It is the same way with your focus on your calling or gifting, you have to call out to it in order for it to present itself and come closer. You call out to it, you draw it closer with your rope of action, and it will begin to draw you closer to it as well. It will run to you.

Anytime you call for a dog to "Come," it will begin to come closer to you. But you must call it. You must put the action behind your vocal cords and call that dog to come to you, and it will begin to come. If you say, "Kitty, kitty, kitty," the cat begins to come closer to you. That's your action. You are doing something about it to draw it closer to you in your life.

POWER OF SURRENDER

The last point I want to bring to you is the lack of surrender. The lack of surrender means that you are not willing to give into what God has for you to do, and what it is going to do for you. You have to surrender to the call of God on your life. You have to surrender to the gift, and let it make room inside of you to do what it needs to do, to take you where you need to go, and grow within you as you grow in it.

When you surrender that means you have been made pliable. You have made it a place and you can give in to it. I didn't say give in to other people, give into other people's opinions, give into the obstacle; all these things you cannot give into. But you must give in to a place of surrender: Surrender before God, and surrender to your gift, surrender to your object of affection.

When a man and woman get married they have to surrender. When the man asks the woman to marry him, there is a surrendering process to say, "Yes, I will marry you." This means, "Yes, I surrender. I don't give up everything that I am, but I surrender to be flexible to move in your life. I surrender to move with you. I surrender now to make decisions with you. I surrender to grow old together. I surrender that we will make it through the obstacles of the tough times of disagreement. I surrender that we will be okay when you forget to put the cap on the toothpaste, or leaving the commode seat up. I surrender to you that through the funny, the silly, the serious things of life, we will work through them together. My surrendering is we will run this race together. We will go through every trial, every good, and every bad, every positive and every negative thing together. I surrender out of a place of trusting."

You have to surrender in the same way to the call of God within you, "I surrender, God, to the presence of this mighty corporation you are creating in me... I surrender to this powerful business that is about to be incorporated... I surrender to the call of being a teacher... I surrender to this gift that you have placed upon me."

When you do this you open-up the airwaves to allow that object, that gift, that goal that call to begin to have its way. You give it legal access, from the Kingdom of God, to begin to grow and to be and to do whatever it needs to be and do. You will never truly see the outcome of it until you reach that point of full surrender in your life.

Remember, life is about faith. You may not know what the finished outcome will look like at the beginning. But you can see it develop by feeding into it, nurturing it, watering it, and imagine what it could possibly look like at the end.

Always allow the expansion to have its way in you. That's a place of surrender, allowing it to happen the way it desires to happen. And you feed into its growth by saying, "I know it's going to be big. I am going to have nine or ten stores. I know we're going to turn around not only clothes, but also jewelry. I know it will be so big, that I will have companies call upon me to ask me how to help them out in my venture. I surrender to it." So you feed into it the creativity to be what it needs to be and have its way within your life. That's the place you move into.

APPRECIATION AND VALUE

The very last thing is to make sure that you never have a lack of appreciation. When you stop appreciating the call, you forget the value, the respect and the integrity that God has put into it. You have to be careful to never take away from the thankfulness and the appreciation of what your gift has done, what it will do, and what it will continue to do for you as you continue to give that same appreciation to it.

"Rejoice always, pray without ceasing, in everything give thanks; for this is the will of God in Christ Jesus for you." 1 Thessalonians 5:16-18

Make sure you feed the appreciation of any goal, any prize, and any race that God has brought to you; bring forth the appreciation. The lack of thankfulness, the lack of appreciation, the lack of flexibility, the lack of giving it credibility, the lack of all of these things will ultimately stunt its growth and destroy you.

You can never succeed in any goal and allow it to be what it is supposed to be if you don't feed it with a thankful heart. Always be grateful for anything and everything that God brings to you, any idea that says, "Now run the race with it. Let me see what you can do with it. Let me see you grow it. Let Me see the expansion of what happens when My co-creator son or daughter unravels the mystery of it, begins to take the now off the present, and begins to run with it. Let Me see what you can feed into it with your imagination. Let Me see how powerful the two of you can be together with your gift or your entrepreneurship, or your business or your teaching ability, etc. Let Me see what you and that gift or that focus or that object can do together when you begin to complement one another, appreciate one another, love one another, and be thankful for one another."

ONLY YOU CAN DECIDE

In stepping into your calling and career, you must pay attention. Focus on your gift. The more you focus on it, the more you will empower it, and the more it will grow for you. Remember, whenever you feed into something it will feed back into you. That's a universal law: whenever you feed into something, it will feed back into you. Always feed it love, appreciation, respect, integrity and excellence and it will give you back the same exact thing.

"Cast your bread upon the waters, For you will find it after many days." Ecclesiastes 11:1

Which means you cast it out there to say, "I appreciate you, and I send my words of appreciation to you. I cast my words of thankfulness to you, gift. I send my words of appreciation of this mighty business I will have some day," and it returns back to you and says, "I remember when you appreciated me. When you fed into me. When you watered me as a business. When you fed into me, as far as a future business deal, I remember what you gave to me. Now I am returning the favor and I'm giving you more than what you even put into me."

Whatever you put out there as a seed, it will grow and it will expand. Get ready to see the expansion of your thanksgiving coming your way in your life. Remember daily to pay attention to detail. Pay attention and focus on the drive that God has placed in you today.

So decide today, where is your life?

Where is right now in the present?

Where is your life headed?

Where is it going from here?

Is it going the same path as far as continuing what you're doing?

I beg you, don't look back fifteen years from now and say, "I'm doing the same old thing that I hate doing." You'll realize that your life was miserable. Your life was never adventurous, it was never on a journey, it was never full of faith, it was never something where you said, and "I love my life."

*"I call heaven and earth to witness this day against you that I have set before you life and death, the blessings and the curses; **therefore choose life**, that you and your descendants may live." Deuteronomy 30:19*

Take a look at your life today. If there need to be changes, guess who needs to make the changes? Not your parents, not your neighbors, but you. You have the you have the power in you to choose life or death. I would say to you today, choose life. Choose the thing that has been after you since the moment you opened your eyes and and before you entered your mother's womb.

Something has been drawing you. It is time. Your time is here. It is your time today. Take that step of faith, move into it, and be who you are called to be in life.

BIO OF
DR. JEREMY LOPEZ:

Dr. Jeremy Lopez is Founder and President of **Identity Network International, Sounds for Now, Awakening to Your Now** and **Now is Your Moment.** Identity Network is a prophetic resource website that reaches well over 153,000 people around the globe and distributes books and teaching CD's. Jeremy has taught and prophesied to thousands of people from all walks of life such as local church congregations, producers, investors, business owners, attorneys, city leaders, musicians, and various ministries around the world concerning areas such as finding missing children, financial breakthroughs, parenthood, and life changing decisions.

Dr. Jeremy Lopez is an international teacher and motivational speaker. Dr. Jeremy speaks on new dimensions of revelatory knowledge in scripture, universal laws, mysteries, patterns, and cycles. He has a love for all people and desires to enrich their lives with love, grace and the mercy of God and to empower them to be successful. Dr. Jeremy believes it is time to awake the Christ Conscious mind and live out the victorious life that was meant for us. His desire is to live a life filled with purpose, potential, and destiny. He ministers with a revelational prophetic teaching gift that brings a freshness of the word of the Lord to people everywhere.

This is accomplished through conferences, prophetic meetings, and seminars. He serves on many governing boards, speaks to business leaders across the nation, and also holds a Doctorate of Divinity. He has had the privilege of ministering prophetically to Governor Bob Riley of Alabama. He has also ministered to thousands overseas including millionaires around the world. He has traveled to many nations including Jamaica, Prague, Paris, Indonesia, Haiti, Hong Kong, Taiwan, UK, Mexico, Singapore, Bahamas, Costa Rica, Puerto Rico, etc. He has hosted and been a guest on several radio and TV programs from Indonesia to New York.

He is the author of nationally published books, 'The Laws of Financial Progression,' 'The Power of the Eternal Now' (Destiny Image) and his newest book, 'Releasing the Power of the Prophetic' (Chosen Books). He has also recorded over 45 teaching CD's.

Jeremy's ministry has been recognized by many national leaders and other prophetic leaders around the nation.

For more information on Dr. Jeremy Lopez, please visit www.DrJeremyLopez.com.

Dr. Jeremy Lopez has many books, e-books, audio downloads, and teaching CDs for you to enjoy and to grow.

OTHER PRODUCT BY DR. LOPEZ:

Books:

Abandoned To Divine Destiny:
You Were Before Time (book)
by Jeremy Lopez

The Power of the Eternal Now (book)
by Jeremy Lopez

The Laws of Financial Progression (book)
by Dr. Jeremy Lopez

Releasing the Power of the Prophetic:
A Practical Guide to Developing a Listening Ear and
Discerning Spirit (book)
by Jeremy Lopez

Made in the USA
Columbia, SC
13 March 2023

13704384R00048